W9-CSM-501

Musician

Peggy J. Parks

KIDHAVEN PRESS™

THOMSON

GALE

San Dieg   and
New Ha   ich

© 2004 by KidHaven Press. KidHaven Press is an imprint of The Gale Group, Inc., a division of Thomson Learning, Inc.

KidHaven™ and Thomson Learning™ are trademarks used herein under license.

For more information, contact
KidHaven Press
27500 Drake Rd.
Farmington Hills, MI 48331-3535
Or you can visit our Internet site at http://www.gale.com

LIBRARY OF CONGRESS CATALOGING-IN-PUBLICATION DATA

Parks, Peggy J., 1951-
  Musician / by Peggy J. Parks.
    v. cm.—(Exploring careers)
Includes bibliographical references and index.
Contents: Kinds of musicians—What it takes to be a musician—What musicians do—Meet a musician.
  ISBN 0-7377-2067-0 (hardback : alk. paper)
  1. Music—Vocational guidance—Juvenile literature. 2. Musicians—Juvenile literature. [1. Music—Vocational guidance. 2. Vocational guidance.] I. Title. II. Exploring careers (KidHaven Press)
  ML3795.P37 2004
  780'.23—dc22
                                                                 2003016267

Printed in the United States of America

CONTENTS

CHAPTER 1

Different Kinds of Musicians

Anyone who makes and performs music is considered a musician. Some play instruments, others sing, and many do both. There are those who manage to climb the ladder of success and become rich and famous—but that is rare, as British folk musician Jacey Bedford explains: "Only a tiny proportion of people working in the music business are famous, and even with them it can be a here today, gone tomorrow thing. The musicians who have a long career are those whose ambition is to be good, not to be famous."[1]

Professional musicians like Bedford have chosen music as their career. For them, music is not just something they do for fun. It is also how they earn their living.

Musicians may specialize in a certain kind of music, or they may perform a variety of different types. Jazz drummers, opera singers, country-western

A small number of musicians become rich and famous. Many others, like this saxophonist, play because they love to share their music.

fiddlers, and blues guitarists are all examples of musicians. There are big-band musicians as well as rap, ragtime, and reggae musicians. Some perform classical Bach, while others lean toward classic rock. Many musicians are also **composers**, which means they create their own music. Some composers also create music for other musicians to perform.

Musicians who work at recording studios and play backup music for singers and groups are known

Pianists perform at a piano bar. Many people go out to hear live music.

as **session** (or studio) **musicians**. Russ Miller is a session musician who has played drums for many top stars and has been featured on hundreds of recordings. Miller says that the most successful session musicians are proficient in a number of different styles. He calls this being "convincing," as he explains: "Eventually, certain **gigs** [concerts] that you do and certain people and circles that you're in are going to dictate what you do well and specialize in. But if you're trying to make a living, get convincing in as many styles as possible."[2]

Session musicians also play music that is featured in movies and television shows, as well as in commercials. Guitarist Michael Batio has performed in commercials for Burger King, Pizza Hut, Taco Bell, McDonald's, and KFC (Kentucky Fried Chicken), among others.

One unusual type of musician is the **turntablist**, who is also called a DJ (disc jockey). The instrument played by these musicians is actually a record player. As a vinyl record spins on the turntable, DJs use the phonograph needle to scratch the record, which creates many unique sounds. One well-known DJ is Mike Gunn. More commonly known as Mix Master Mike, Gunn performs with the hip-hop group Beastie Boys.

The Same (but Different)

Most musicians know how to read music, but not all of them use it when they perform. One type of

A DJ scratches out a tune on his turntable.

musician who absolutely must use sheet music is the orchestra member. People who play with symphony orchestras pay close attention to sheet music during performances. That is because the music they play is designed for many different instruments, and all the harmonies and melodies must blend together perfectly. According to Carter Brey, a cellist with the New York Philharmonic, this can be challenging for orchestra members. They must understand the music and know exactly how their parts fit into it. Also, each musician in a particular section—such as the cellos—must pay close attention to the music played by other members of the section, as Brey explains: "A lot of my responsibilities [as **principal** cellist] have to do with making sure that we're all pulling the oar the right way. There has to be a kind of blend, and I'm responsible for that."[3] Timing is also important for orchestra members. During their performances, they must time their entrances and exits perfectly. Also, while they are performing they must pay close attention to the conductor, whose job is to lead the orchestra.

Making It Up

Unlike musicians who play in orchestras, some musicians do not perform in such a precise, disciplined way. For instance, jazz musicians often **improvise**, which means they change the music while they are playing it. Even if they play the same song over and over again, it will probably sound a bit different each time. Jazz trumpeter Marvin Stamm describes improvisation as a musical language. When musicians perform together, they use the language to "talk" to each other through their instruments. He explains how the process works: "If I desire, I can change the 'feel' and setting of the piece. For instance, I can play a composition in bossa nova style one evening and the next evening play it in a 'swing' style. Even if they continue to play a piece in the same style, most creative Jazz musicians strive not to be repetitive.

They are always searching for new ways to express themselves and expand their ideas and skills of communicating."[4] Other musicians enjoy improvising as well. For example, members of rock and country-western bands rarely play songs exactly the same way when they perform.

Whether their specialty is strumming a guitar or blowing a trumpet, plucking a harp or playing a harpsichord, musicians' lives revolve around music. Their styles and techniques may be totally different,

Jazz musicians try to make each performance different. They often change the music as they play it.

Talent and a sincere love of music make *N SYNC one of the world's most successful pop bands.

but there is one thing they all share in common: a love of music. Because of that, they have chosen music for their careers—and most of them could not imagine doing anything else.

CHAPTER 2

What It Takes to Be a Musician

Most musicians realize the importance of talent. Some talent, such as a beautiful singing voice or the ability to play instruments, may come naturally. However, it takes many years of work to develop talent to a professional level. Jacey Bedford talks about what it takes to make it in the world of professional music: "You can decide to go pro and make a career plan, but unless you've got two essential ingredients, talent and determination, you won't make it work."[5] Musicians must be motivated to work hard at improving their skills. Most say that no matter how good they become, they always keep trying to be better.

When it comes to education and training, no two musicians are exactly the same. Those who perform

Symphonic orchestras rehearse countless hours to improve their performances.

with symphony orchestras or operas almost always have college degrees, as well as extensive training in classical music. Many musicians have studied for years at music schools and/or with private instructors. For example, Tori Amos has had years of formal musical training that started when she was very young. By the time she was six, she was studying classical piano at the famed Peabody Institute in Baltimore. She was the youngest student ever to attend the school.

Not all musicians have formal training, however. Some have developed their natural talent and skills through years of self-instruction and practice. Russ Miller says that most musicians end up being their own best teachers. But he still stresses the importance of formal training, and he explains why: "The reason is that if you don't have proper technique—particularly with a very physical instrument like drums—you're going to get led down a path where it becomes difficult to play certain things once you reach a certain level."[6] Miller says one result of improper playing techniques is the risk of injury. He has known drummers and guitar players who have injured their wrists in this way. They must wear wrist braces much of the time, and they often find performing to be painful.

Self-Confidence

Whether they play instruments or sing, musicians must believe in themselves and their abilities. Some are confident by nature, while others are not. Yet even though it may be difficult, everyone who performs professionally must work at developing self-confidence. This includes overcoming stage fright, which can be a problem for any musician who performs live.

Musicians must also be able to handle rejection. Successful musicians are those people who have the

A music class works to perfect a piece. Some musicians have years of formal instruction while others teach themselves to play.

willingness and the courage to keep trying—even when it would be easier to give up. According to music publicist Ariel Hyatt, facing rejection is just part of being a musician: "Trying to make a living making music is not for the meek. If you are not willing to work very hard and have a lot of doors slammed in your face, don't try to make a go of this . . . and if you can accept this and plow forward taking risks and not taking no for an answer, things will begin to happen."[7]

Coping with Unpredictability

Rejection is not the only tough part of being a musician. They also have to live lives that can be stressful and unpredictable. For instance, musicians who spend a lot of time touring can be away from home for months at a time. They hop from city to city and from hotel to hotel, which can be frustrating. John McCrea, lead singer for the rock group Cake, describes how unglamorous and difficult touring can be: "If anyone thinks it's easy to do, let them leave their homes and families and everything else they know for two years and then come back to discuss it with me. . . . For a while, it's great to go out and play in front of people who clearly want to hear you. But then you realize it's the exact same thing night after night, and you feel less like an 'artist' and more like one of those performing bears at Chuck E Cheese."[8]

Even musicians who do not tour have to cope with strange hours. Those who perform in night-

The band Cake performs on tour. Musicians sometimes spend a long time away from home and have difficult schedules.

clubs and theaters usually work at night and are often not finished performing until 2:00 A.M. or later. Musicians who perform with operas or symphony orchestras also endure unpredictable schedules. Flutist Mindy Kaufman works five or six days per week with the New York Philharmonic. She rehearses with the orchestra about twenty hours a week and performs in concerts three or four nights a week. She shares her thoughts on the schedule challenges faced by musicians: "We work on Saturday

Street musicians like these depend on their audience to give them money.

nights and almost every holiday—if you don't want to work on holidays, if you want to go away on the weekends, you shouldn't be a musician."[9]

Another unpredictable aspect of a musician's life is income, which can fluctuate radically. Musicians' earnings depend on many factors. Those who perform in small, local clubs may earn only a few hundred dollars per performance. Well-known musicians who perform in large clubs and resorts may earn thousands of dollars, and those who become famous may earn millions. When they are just starting out, most musicians are unable to earn enough money to make a living. So, they often work at other jobs until their music careers take off.

All musicians, whether they play instruments or sing, are unique in their own way. Their career paths are often different, as are their education and training. But there are qualities they all share, such as talent, a commitment to work hard, and a willingness to accept the bad with the good. That is what makes them professional. That is what makes them succeed. And that is what makes them musicians.

CHAPTER 3

What Musicians Do

Young people who dream about becoming professional musicians may think only about the magic of being on stage. However, a musician's career is about more than just performing. It also involves a tremendous amount of work. Many of them continue studying music even after they have become professional musicians. They also practice and rehearse on a regular basis. Those who tour spend hours traveling from one place to another. Sometimes musicians have so much to do that their lives are unbelievably hectic.

Creating New Music

Musicians who write their own music spend a great deal of time creating it. No two musicians follow exactly the same steps because there is no "right" way to compose music. Some musicians start by writing their ideas on paper. They create **scores**, which are musical charts that show the different parts of the music. Other musicians create music on electronic instruments called **synthesizers**.

No matter what process they use, most musicians say it starts with an inspiration. Curtis S.D. Macdonald, a composer from California, shares his thoughts on creating music: "All types of music can

Bruce Springsteen takes a break during a concert tour to write a new song.

be composed, and composers, through hard work and training, can create anything they hear in their head . . . music that can tug at your heart or music that scares you to death."[10] Macdonald says composing is similar to building with Legos of different sizes and shapes. The farther he goes along, the more his music takes shape. His first step is to sketch the music on paper, which gives him an idea of how it will flow. Then he uses his computer to add the sounds of various instruments. As Macdonald works on a piece of music, he may follow his written sketch exactly, or he may improvise. It takes him about thirty minutes to compose one minute's worth of music.

Practice, Practice, Practice

One activity that musicians share in common is regular practice. Practicing helps them play music more smoothly so they are less apt to make errors while performing. Also, those who play instruments depend on certain muscles, and practice helps keep their muscles in shape. Singers practice to exercise their vocal muscles. The time they spend practicing, and the methods they use, often vary. Some play or sing music scales, while others just run through their songs over and over again. Some practice by themselves, while those who play as part of a group may rehearse along with other musicians.

When Mindy Kaufman was in high school, she enjoyed practicing so much that she never thought of it as a chore. Now that she is a professional musician,

Practicing helps musicians improve their playing and keeps their muscles in shape.

she still practices from one to three hours every day. She explains the importance of this: "It's almost like playing tennis, where you have to work on your serve, your backhand, your forehand, the lob—you have all these different shots, and you have to work on all of them because they're all part of the game."[11]

Being Onstage

Musicians invest a great deal of time and energy in their careers. So when they finally get a chance to perform, it is their reward for a lot of hard work.

Most musicians find performing to be the most enjoyable part of what they do, as Jacey Bedford explains: "You can't really beat the feeling of walking out onto a stage and having twelve hundred people leap to their feet cheering. Okay, that doesn't happen every time, but when it does, it makes up for all those times you've played to three people and the theatre cat."[12] Even musicians who perform in smaller

The huge smile on Buffy St. Marie's face shows how much she enjoys singing before a live audience.

Opera singer Jane Eaglen (bottom) warms up her voice before each performance.

venues and clubs enjoy the rush of performing before live audiences.

When musicians are scheduled to perform in the evening, they often spend part of the day preparing. Jane Eaglen, an opera singer in Seattle, warms up her voice by singing scales and singing in the shower. She arrives at the theater about an hour and a half before the show. First, a makeup artist does her makeup. Then she is assisted with her costume and wig. The performance lasts for three hours, and afterwards Eaglen accepts flowers from her fans and signs autographs. She says that most performances go well, but she describes a few times when that was not the case: "I have been in performances where sets fell, curtains came in early, and once I was even kneed between the legs to get me off a high note when the other singer was not happy with the sound he was making, but that is rare!"[13]

The Physical Side

Musicians like Eaglen work in theaters where there are crews to handle equipment and stage setup. However, many musicians handle this themselves, and it can be an exhausting task that takes hours of hard work. Musicians must set up speakers and amplifiers that are often large and heavy. Drums, keyboards, microphones, and guitar stands must be placed in the right position. There are cables to be strung for the sound system, and there is stage lighting to be set up. Once everything is in place, the musicians must do a sound check, or test, to make sure all equipment works properly. After the performance is over, the musicians may leave the equipment if they are performing in the same place the next night. If they are on tour, however, they need to repack everything and load it all into trucks so it can be taken to the next gig. Jeff Abercrombie, bass guitarist for the rock band Fuel, talks about what this was like when his group was just starting out: "Our life consisted of driving to the gig, setting it up, playing our show, breaking down the PA, driving back home. Then doing it all again the next day and just on and on."[14] According to Bedford, her group spends about three hours setting up their equipment for a two-hour performance. Once the show is over, it takes them another hour to tear everything down again.

Getting Attention

Another important task for musicians is booking gigs. Some hire booking agents to handle this, but many do it on their own. This involves keeping in

Many musicians, like singer Ricky Martin, make personal appearances at music stores.

touch with the people who schedule performing acts. Many musicians send out promotional packages, which include information about the band and a sample CD. Then they follow up with a telephone call. Sometimes they must perform a live audition before being booked.

Publicity

Musicians who are well-known or famous usually hire music publicists. However, most musicians handle their own publicity. This involves setting up interviews with radio stations and talking with newspaper and magazine writers. It can also involve scheduling promotional events, such as personal appearances at music stores.

Just as no two musicians are exactly alike, their tasks are different as well. Some practice an hour a day, while others practice for three hours or more. Some perform on the same stage night after night, and others tour the country for half the year. Some have achieved fame, while others only dream about it. Yet no matter who they are or what they spend their time doing, their reward is the same: the chance to share their musical talents with their fans.

CHAPTER 4

Meet a Musician

Nina Storey is a singer and pianist who has performed professionally since she was fifteen years old. She released her first CD in 1993, and over the next ten years she released three more. Throughout her career she has had many exciting opportunities, such as singing backup vocals for the rock group INXS. She has also performed twice in Europe and has toured with blues guitarist and singer Jonny Lang. She has been featured at such major events as the Sundance Film Festival, Lilith Fair, Woodstock '99, and the Monterey Bay Blues Festival. In addition, she has often performed the national anthem for such sports teams as the Chicago Bulls, the Denver Broncos, and the Colorado Avalanche.

Storey says that she has loved music since she was a little girl. "I grew up in a musical family where

Nina Storey sings at the Monterey Bay Blues Festival. She grew up in a musical family.

music was very important. My mom was a song-writer and producer, and my father was a sound engineer. For as long as I can remember, my parents inspired and encouraged me in any musical path I chose to follow."[15] Storey's first experience with a musical instrument was a bit unusual, as she explains: "When I was about six or seven years old, I read a book about a little girl who played the violin. She didn't have an instrument so she made one out of wood. That had such an impression on me—whatever she did, I wanted to do, too. So I mounted pencils on a piece of cardboard, strung rubber bands across the pencils, and then sat there plucking my little homemade violin."[16]

The Road to Success

Storey cannot remember a time when she did not sing:

> Singing has always come naturally to me. I sang around the house all the time, I sang in the glee club in junior high, and when I was in high school I had the awesome chance to do a music video with INXS. Yet no matter how many opportunities I had early on, I really believe the biggest factor in my success was my parents' constant encouragement. They told me I was talented, so I believed I was talented —and if kids are told that at an early age, they are set up to succeed. That was certainly the case with me.[17]

After Storey graduated from high school, she attended college at the University of Colorado at Boulder. During her freshman year, she regularly performed at parties and clubs around the Boulder area. Then she received an exciting offer:

> I had relatives who worked for the USO [United Service Organizations], and they signed me to do a one-month tour in Europe. My sister went along to to play guitar and sing backup, and our first gig was performing at the World's Fair in Seville, Spain. Then they asked me to perform for U.S. soldiers on the aircraft carrier USS *Saratoga*, which was anchored in the middle of the Mediterranean Sea. They actually had to fly us in on fighter jets, and we landed right on the ship! I performed for five thousand U.S. troops. I still remember the thrill of looking around and seeing guys everywhere—even hanging off the towers, taking photos. It was an amazing, incredible experience. [18]

When Storey's European tour was over, she returned to Boulder and went back to school. She continued writing music and performing, and eventually she left college to pursue her musical career full-time.

Memorable Experiences

Like all professional musicians, Storey has interesting stories to tell:

Blues singer Etta James points to her new star on the Hollywood Walk of Fame in Hollywood, California.

One of my most memorable gigs was when I was asked to open for [blues singer] Etta James. It was at a big venue in Denver, and I didn't have a car at the time. So, I packed a long, black satin dress in my backpack and hopped on a bus. I was very nervous because I was the opening act for a singer who has been my idol forever. I performed in front of several thousand people and got a standing ovation at the end, which was thrilling. After I got off stage, I had a terrible stomachache and it kept getting worse. I wanted to meet Etta James so bad, but I had to go backstage and lie down, and the only place available was a smelly room where all the beer kegs were kept. There I was in my black dress, lying on the floor, feeling sick. And I never did get to meet her![19]

Another of Storey's memorable experiences happened during a different Colorado performance:

We were shooting a video, and there was some equipment on the stage that I didn't know was there. The venue was packed completely full, and during my show, I fell over a monitor and ended up upside down with my feet in the air. I couldn't get up—I was just stuck there, wedged in tight. The videotape was rolling, and I heard this gasp from the crowd. Somehow I managed to get myself unstuck, stood up, cracked some jokes, and got back into my performance. What else can you do in a situation like that? You just have to laugh it off.[20]

A Musician's Life

Storey says she loves being a professional musician:

It is really exciting. Whenever I create music, I have this urge to share it with other people. I feel like it's my purpose in life—to share what's inside of me. I think that's natural for anyone, really. When you create something

Musicians never know in advance how a show will turn out.

you love, you want to share it with others. And when I'm onstage, and I hear people clapping and cheering for me—well, there's no way to even describe what that feels like.[21]

The amount of time Storey spends touring can vary. She is especially busy during the summer months because she performs at festivals and events all over the United States. She also spends time in recording sessions and working on publicity with her agent, Jan Storey, who also happens to be her mother.

As for how she spends her time when not onstage, Storey says she sticks to a pretty regular routine. "I spend a lot of time practicing every day. That is an absolute necessity. If I don't sing every day, my muscles remind me. I do vocal exercises, practice sounds and scales. Plus, I play the piano and guitar, so I practice those instruments as well."[22]

Another activity that takes up quite a bit of Storey's time is composing music:

I usually write several songs a week. Sometimes I get an idea for a song, but for one reason or another, it's just not the right time to finish it. So, I just file the idea away, and I might not think about it again for quite a while. This actually happened to me recently. About a year ago, I had an idea for a song about giving people a chance. I wrote the lyrics, but the music wouldn't come together, so I filed the idea away. Then one day I was driving along the

When a musician composes a piece of music, an idea may come from anywhere at any time.

road in Los Angeles, and I saw a homeless man holding a sign. I stopped and talked to him— and suddenly the music came to me. I finished writing the song, and now I'm performing it.[23]

Storey says that human issues such as homelessness often inspire her: "The songs I write help me remember what kind of person I want to be and how I want to live my life. When I perform them, if

Musicians put a lot of time, energy, and work into the thing they love most.

I can help other people connect too—well, that's awesome." [24]

When Storey is scheduled to perform, she does vocal warm-ups for thirty minutes beforehand. She also does vocal exercises after each performance because, as she says, "It's kind of like doing stretching exercises after running in a race." Storey does not talk after she performs—even when she is signing autographs. In fact, she is always conscious of protecting her voice, as she explains: "Even when I'm on a roller coaster, I don't yell! People may not realize that singing is a very physical endeavor. I'm careful with my voice so I don't wear it out."[25]

Message for Aspiring Musicians

Storey says she once heard something at a music conference that inspired her and has helped her throughout her career:

> The speaker said that if you work hard and you love what you do, you may not get to the top of every mountain—but you will reach the top of your own mountain. I have never forgotten that. And that is what I want to pass along to kids. Being a professional musician is wonderful and rewarding and fun. But please keep in mind that it also involves a lot of time, energy, and work. You have to set goals, and you have to stick with them. Learn everything you can about music, and develop your craft. Practice and then practice some more. And most of all, remember to be true to yourself, believe in yourself, and surround yourself with people who believe in you. After all, the only real measure of success is if you are truly happy and fulfilled and feel good about yourself and what you do. With that as your goal, you can't go wrong.[26]

Chapter 1: Different Kinds of Musicians

1. Jacey Bedford, interview by author, February 7, 2002.

2. Quoted in Jake Sibley, "Interview: Russ Miller," *About.com* ("Musicians' Exchange" section). http://musicians.about.com.

3. Quoted in Beth Nissen, "The Players: Career Musicians of the New York Philharmonic," *CNN.com/Career* February 23, 2001. www.cnn.com.

4. Marvin Stamm, "How We Do What We Do," *Jazz 52nd Street.* http://52ndstreet.com/kenton/stamm.htm.

Chapter 2: What It Takes to Be a Musician

5. Bedford, interview.

6. Quoted in Sibley, "Interview."

7. Quoted in Alex Teitz, "Ariel Hyatt: Making a Name for Yourself and for Every Artist." *Articles About Ariel and Ariel Publicity.* www.arielpublicity.com.

8. Quoted in Barnes and Noble, "Devils Food for Thought," July 24, 2001. http://music.barnesand noble.com.

9. Quoted in Beth Nissen, "The Players: Career Musicians of the New York Philharmonic," *CNN. com/Career* February 23, 2001. www.cnn.com.

Chapter 3: What Musicians Do

10. Curtis S.D. Macdonald, interview by author, February 13, 2002.

11. Quoted in Nissen, "Flutist Mindy Kaufman."

12. Bedford, interview.

13. Jane Eaglen, "Diary: A Weeklong Electronic Journal," *Slate*, October 22, 2001. http://slate.msn.com.

14. Quoted in Jodi Summers, *Making & Marketing Music*. New York: Allworth Press, 1999, p. 44.

Chapter 4: Meet a Musician

All quotes in Chapter 4: Nina Storey, interview by author, June 30, 2003.

GLOSSARY

composer: Someone who creates a piece of music.

gig: A commonly used slang term for a concert or performance.

improvise: Making up music or changing it on the spot, rather than following the way it was written originally.

principal: The leading player in an orchestra or section.

score: A musical composition in written form.

session musicians: Musicians who work at recording studios and play backup music for other singers and groups.

synthesizer: An instrument that generates musical sounds electronically.

turntablist: A musician who uses the turntable and needle of a record player to create different sounds (also called a DJ).

venue: A specific location, such as where a concert or performance is held.

FOR FURTHER EXPLORATION

Books

Craig Awmiller, *Wynton Marsalis: Gifted Trumpet Player*. New York: Childrens Press, 1996. A story of the life and career of Wynton Marsalis, an African American musician who plays both jazz and classical music. Also discusses his fondness for teaching children about music.

Robert T. Levine, *The Story of the Orchestra: Listen While You Learn About the Instruments, the Music, and the Composers Who Wrote the Music*. New York: Black Dog & Leventhal, 2001. The author, who calls himself "Orchestra Bob," teaches readers about musical periods, famous composers, and various instruments.

Diane Lindsey Reeves, *Career Ideas for Kids Who Like Music and Dance*. New York: Checkmark Books, 2001. An informative book designed for young people who are interested in pursuing musical careers.

Harvey R. Snitkin, *Practicing for Young Musicians: You Are Your Own Teacher*. Niantic, CT: HMS, 1997. Includes techniques designed to help aspiring musicians get more benefits and enjoyment out of regular practice.

Leslie Strudwick, *Musicians*. New York: Crabtree, 1998. Describes the lives and achievements of six female musicians, including a composer, a classical guitarist, a violinist, and others.

Stephen Webber, *Turntable Technique: The Art of the DJ*. Boston: Berklee Press, 1999. The story of turntablists and the changes they have made in the music industry. Includes photographs, exercises, and interviews with top DJs.

Websites

Music Education at DataDragon (http://datadragon.com/education). Includes easy instructions on how to read music, information about music history, and a message board for music-related questions.

Music Notes (http://library.thinkquest.org/15413). Information about music theory, history, styles, and careers. Also includes descriptions of musical instruments, as well as interactive games for music lovers.

New York Philharmonic Kidzone (www.nyphilkids.org/main.phtml). Site visitors can meet composers and members of the orchestra, learn about different instruments, learn how to invent their own instrument, read music news, and play games.

Pay the Piper (www.paythepiper.co.uk). A wonderful collection of music-related information for young people and parents. Describes a variety of instruments and includes advice about how to choose and buy them and about practicing, lessons, and other topics.

INDEX

ABOUT THE AUTHOR

Peggy J. Parks holds a bachelor of science degree from Aquinas College in Grand Rapids, Michigan, where she graduated magna cum laude. She is a freelance writer and author who has written a number of books for various Gale Group imprints, including KidHaven Press, Blackbirch Press, and Lucent Books. Parks lives in Muskegon, Michigan, a town that she says inspires her writing because of its location on the shores of Lake Michigan.